Someone
Somewhere
Maybe

Someone Somewhere Maybe

Poems

SOPHIE DIENER

With illustrations by
Chloe Purpero Johnson

ST. MARTIN'S GRIFFIN
NEW YORK

First published in the United States by St. Martin's Griffin, an imprint of St. Martin's Publishing Group

SOMEONE SOMEWHERE MAYBE. Copyright © 2023 by Sophie Diener. Illustrations copyright © 2023 by Chloe Purpero Johnson. All rights reserved. Printed in the United States of America. For information, address St. Martin's Publishing Group, 120 Broadway, New York, NY 10271.

www.stmartins.com

The Library of Congress Cataloging-in-Publication Data is available upon request.

ISBN 978-1-250-89271-3 (trade paperback)
ISBN 978-1-250-89272-0 (ebook)

Our books may be purchased in bulk for promotional, educational, or business use. Please contact your local bookseller or the Macmillan Corporate and Premium Sales Department at 1-800-221-7945, extension 5442, or by email at MacmillanSpecialMarkets@macmillan.com.

First Edition: 2023

10 9 8 7 6 5 4 3 2 1

Contents

Preface

My first journal was pale pink and princess themed. Every other page was blank so there was space to draw pictures. In this journal I learned that if I wrote down my memories, I could remember them more. I liked to remember.

Later, I was given a box that neatly held twelve notebooks, each one labeled with the name of a month. These journals are filled now with big feelings from middle school. Some of the pages were even torn out by my eighth-grade self because I was so embarrassed by them. But with these journals, I learned that writing could make me feel better. And I liked to feel better.

At some point I started writing song lyrics, and then song lyrics turned into poems. I have written when I've been anxious, happy, heartbroken, angry, scared, grateful, completely in love, and content. I have written about real things that have happened to me, and I have written made-up stories that reflect feelings I've only imagined.

I've always loved to write, and I've also loved to read. Over and over again, my heart has been soothed by art that has moved me to whisper, "You, too?"

In *Someone Somewhere Maybe*, I wrote to remember. I wrote to remember how it felt to be seventeen and twenty-three—heartbroken and in love and in between. I often wrote in an attempt to feel better. I wrote to untangle the intangible—all of the anxiety and all of the joy. One of my biggest hopes in sharing this collection is that some of these words can become for someone else what others' art has been for me: a reminder that other people feel this way, too; a small light during a long night.

I'm grateful for the way that writing helps me move through this world. The fact that I get to share my writing in this way means so much to every version of me that I have been and that I will be in the future. I'm hopeful you'll find pieces of yourself hidden in these pages, too.

Someone
Somewhere
Maybe

Haunted House

Your house is yellow,
and mine is all white.
I get off the bus,
throw my backpack inside,
and then get on my bike
'cause I'll see you at 3
at the brick house where our two streets meet.
And Jake says it's haunted,
but I think he lied.
Still we won't risk it;
we don't go inside,
but we play in the backyard
'til we hear your dad's car.
I'll see you tomorrow;
goodnight.

Then everything changes
when we turn sixteen
and I trade my bike
for your passenger seat.
And I've never noticed,
but your eyes are so green,
and you seem kind of nervous

when you bring up homecoming,
so we fall in love.
No one's surprised,
except for us.
Then the summer after senior year,
you help me pack my bags in the trunk.
We figure after thirteen years,
eight semesters apart
isn't really that much.
But we're in different time zones,
and when I call you, your voice sounds
rushed.

The next time that I see you,
you don't look at me the same.
When I fly back to college,
there are so many pictures to put away.
The last time I cry over you
is one year later
when I hear her name.
But I get my degree
and rent a house in the city
and everything turns out okay.

Now I'm back in town to see my parents,
and the brick house on their street
has brand-new windows
and the lights are on
and everything looks so clean.

My mom says your name kind of softly
that night at dinner when I ask who bought it,
and I think maybe Jake was right
when he told me that old house
was haunted.

Something So Real

We used to sit on the roof of my car
with legs through the sunroof and eyes toward the stars,
and we'd talk about God and what might be beyond
the walls of the hills we were living between.
We haven't done that in a year, but we're back in our spot,
and my hair is cut shorter, and your eyes are looking off.
There's lake water on your skin,
and tan lines are on your feet
from those strappy shoes you always wear
no matter what you're doing.
We sit there on a blanket by the water
and you say to me,
I think—
you take a breath—
I think this really isn't working.
It's sunset.
You texted me at noon and asked if we could meet
right after I got back in town
here because it's down the street
from where I live;
you hadn't wanted me to drive while I was upset.
You look different—
resigned,

somewhat relieved to have surrendered
to your head.
I say, *Okay, I understand,*
then I cry and you don't.
I whisper, *Hey, feel free to go;*
I'm okay walking home alone.
I have cruel words in my throat,
but I know I don't mean them,
so I stop them in their tracks
instead of letting them follow as you're leaving.
I was the one who showed you this place,
but the waves might as well be whispering your name.
The sky takes your side—there's no thunder or rain,
just pink clouds and orange light
and the ending of another day.
I'm young,
and I don't know it yet,
but I'll be grateful for the memories up
on that car.
I'll be glad that we had something so real
it got to break my heart.

Mean It

I know my memory is not always honest,
but I could have sworn you had made me a promise.
The words in that letter—
didn't you write those?
Wasn't that your voice
coming from my phone?
Weren't you there, too?
Don't you remember?
Midnight in summer,
winter in your sweater,
the backyard,
my birthday,
the lake frozen solid,
the CDs,
the secrets,
the Sundays,
the fog, and the
love.
Wasn't there love?
Did it really happen
or did I just dream it?
Didn't you say it?

Didn't you feel it?
Didn't you mean it?

Didn't you mean it?

I'll Think of You

I'll think of you
when I get caught
in early summer storms.
I'll remember how
the rain leaked through the sunroof
before I finally got it fixed
and drenched
the fabric of the seat
and changed
the color of your jeans
from light to dark.
I'd apologize,
and you'd say,
Please don't start.
There's nowhere that I'd rather be
than with you in your messed-up car.
I'd laugh and drive around to try
to find a place to park.
And we'd run down the battery
of my dented '04 SUV,
letting a scratched antique-store DVD
play dimly on the backseat screen.

A white crop top with unraveling seams
and a damp swimsuit still underneath.
Beach-bleached hair and sunburnt cheeks.
3 A.M.
Empty streets.
I'll try my hardest not to think of you,
then I'll feel sad when I start to forget. I'll wish
I could get these memories out of my head
but find some other place to keep them,
like a box beneath my bed locked
with a key that I can't find,
because then I wouldn't have to relive them
but at least I'd know
they're alive.

Even After

I'm scared I'll

move to a new city
and reach all of my dreams
and learn to be kind to myself
and talk out all my feelings

and be patient with my heart
and trust that time will heal all wounds
and stop looking you up to see
if you've found someone new

and put in work to heal
and look ahead instead of back
and realize in the end that I
still love you

even after all of that.

Eighteen

To the me I was at eighteen,
what I'd give to hold your face in between
my hands
and promise you it's okay.
No one is mad at you.
You don't know what you don't know.
You'll do the best that you can.
In a heartbeat, I swear I'd erase
all your shame.
I know that you can't see it,
but you're growing beautifully.
You're learning how to live with
grace and patience and humility.
Your heart is getting wider,
and you are becoming kinder,
and you're sowing seeds
for all the dreams
that will come true
so soon.

Let me dispel your biggest fear:
I am so proud of you.

A Heart with Legs

You are like a heart
with feet and hands
and legs and arms.
Always feeling things so deeply
must be
hard.

But oh, how beautiful—
your refusal
to let that drain your love,
to let your windows be nailed shut,
to let your doors be boarded up.

Feelings

Your feelings are not right or wrong;
they just *are*. They exist.
Acknowledge them.
Invite them in
for tea.
Send them on their way
when you
are ready.
You don't need
to assign shame or guilt
to natural reactions.
If you're wondering their cause, then
pause and ask them.
Untangle them and name them.
You don't have to run and hide.
It may appear a daunting task,
but you are brave enough to try.
You are capable of recognizing them
within your own good time.
You're capable of facing them
and coming out the other side.

Blue

I asked you,
If I were a color,
what do you think I'd be?
And you didn't even hesitate
before you said,
Green,
like the forest,
like breathing,
like being alive.
And I said
that you would be
blue like the sky—
sort of muted as the summer sun sets
and the radio plays
and my skin smells like sunscreen and smoke.
Blue like my favorite days.
Then you said you loved me
for the very first time.
And I know you meant it
despite how, down the line,
I sit
on ugly linoleum floor
and hear the hum of the fridge

and the lock of the door.
And my tears are hot
as they roll down my cheeks,
as they pool by my feet,
as your car starts and you leave.
You abandon a sweatshirt and give back the spare key
but take the bands I showed you and the way I make my
    coffee.
And I keep reading your favorite book—
the one I swore I would not like—
and when I finally close its cover,
it's all filled with underlines.
There are parts of you that fade with time
then parts of you that stay,
and I'm not sure if you rubbed off on me
or just uncovered what had been hidden away.
Regardless, I think you are so good—
I know now that I was just not meant for you—
and at the end of the day,
I am honored to walk away
a little more blue.

Don't Be a Stranger

You smile weakly and say to me,
Don't be a stranger,
and I nod my head knowing that's what I'll become.
Still there will always be something between us—
a quiet recognition of what once was.

I'm grateful to have known you
in this precious part of your life
and for our paths to have intertwined
for a brief but beautiful time.

Despite the hurt I'm feeling now as it ends,
I know I would love you all over again.
I know I'd let myself be swept up by magic
even if now I can't have it.

One day, when I don't feel hurt anymore,
I'll probably run into you in the store.
You'll be older and wiser and married with kids.
I'll be happy for you,
and I know that I'll get it,

but here in the present I'm breaking
as I let you go,
as you drive away
and I walk the block home,
believing somewhere deep inside me it's right,
even if now I can't understand why.

Have Hope

This is a reminder
if you are in the midst
of a tough transition:
the fact that you miss parts of what you had
doesn't mean you made a bad decision.
Sometimes you'll make choices
good and right and true to who
you are,
and yet as you carry them out,
life might start to feel kind of hard.
You move across the country for your dream job,
and it's not like what you thought.
You leave a relationship
just to feel lonely and lost.
Your new city feels too big,
and that makes you feel really small.

You risked a lot on this,
and now you're scared
you were wrong.

I know it's difficult
to feel like you're just hanging in the in-between

of the foggy future
and the past that was
familiar
at the very least.
So cry your tears
and call your mom
and play sad music
and scream along
and slowly, gently, kindly
learn the words to a new song:
have hope.
You are learning;
you are growing.
Things take time to fall into place,
but you will find the reason you're here.
Light will be woven in as you wait.
And one day,
you'll wake up and have yourself to thank
for trusting that wide-eyed version of you
who knew they needed to take
that first leap of faith.

Meant to Be

You let me have your jacket
when we sat
beside the door
and people flew inside with flushed cheeks
leaving snow prints on the floor.
All the lights were dim and golden
and the black mug spread some warmth
back through my chest,
until I couldn't see my breath.

Two people in the corner set up microphones and their
    guitars.
When you leaned toward the table, you could probably
    hear my heart.
You spoke so quietly,
like every word was just for me,
and my jaw hurt from smiling,
and everything
around froze like the white frost on your Jeep.

I am so happy
I have memories like this to keep.
I don't know where you are

or who you're with
or if you're everything you hoped you'd be.
But those moments are so rare, I think,
where it all connects
so seamlessly—
things do not have to last forever
to have been meant to be.

Who Are You

Who are you
when not held up to
others' expectations?
Who are you
without the fear
of disappointment on their faces?
What do you want
in this life
when you stop looking at it from
the outside?
Which dreams belong to
your mind?

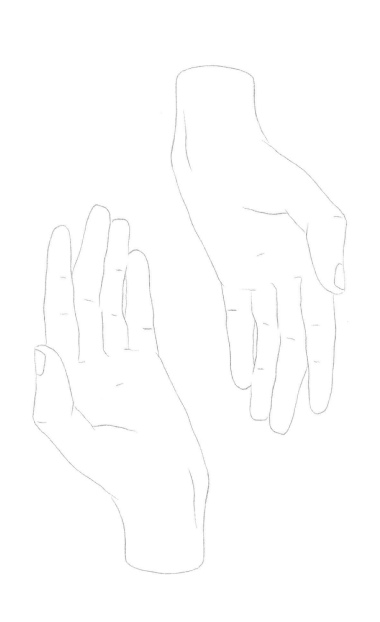

I Hope Today Is Kind to You

I hope today that, if it rains,
it doesn't make it hard to drive.
I hope you get the window seat
at sunrise on your flight,
and that when you look at your crush across the room,
you see they were already looking at you.
I hope you don't get blisters from
your shoes.

I hope your water bottle doesn't fall
and make that clanging sound,
and I hope that, if it does,
it's when nobody is around.
I hope you find a five-dollar bill in your pocket
that you'd forgotten you had.
I hope when you go to watch videos on YouTube,
you only get skippable ads.

I hope you discover a new favorite song.
I hope your weekend takes its time
and that your stomach hurts from laughing too hard
and the sunset glows red through your blinds.
I hope that light shines bright on you

and that you are a source of it for someone else, too.
I hope today—
this week, this year, this life—
is kind to you.

The Last Thing You Have Left to Let Go

There are nine cracks in the sidewalk
in between your house
and mine.
I swear I could get there with my eyes
    closed
after being spun three times.
From five years old
and all through school
the best love that I ever knew
was you—
your hair a mess,
your eyes so blue.

The day you got accepted,
we were lying on the ground.
You opened up the letter,
and your silence spoke so loud.
You're ready to move mountains
and get out of our small town,
and I'm so proud.
You mean it when you say
we'll work it out, but then

you cut your hair
and change your clothes
and start loving songs
that I don't know.
And I know you're not coming home;
I'm the last thing you have left to let go.
And I know that you love me still.
I know that you always will,
but nine cracks in the sidewalk
turns to long drives
turns to late nights
turns to missed calls.

So the next time that I see you,
I put on my bravest face,
and I watch the most beautiful heart I have ever known
hear my words
and break.
And I think about taking it all back
and fighting my way through the airport gates,
but what happens then
when we still don't want the same things in the end?

I buy that house between ours
with the yard we used to meet in.
I know it has its problems,
but there's still potential—
I can see it.
Your parents give me updates on you

when I see them out next door,
and one day—
slowly,
finally—
I don't feel so sad anymore.
The sidewalk gets resurfaced,
and the windows get replaced.
It doesn't hurt the same as it used to—
swearing I hear you out back while I paint.
I'm still kind of nervous that one day
I'll have kids, and they'll run inside, and tell me,
We just saw a ghost
with long blond hair
and bright blue eyes.

Can We Still Be Friends?

You said I could have all of you
or absolutely none,
and so we don't stay friends
or keep in touch,
but just quietly learn how to fall out of love.
And I respect the way you let me go with such
finality—
no second thoughts or midnight calls,
just scissors cutting through strings.
And for a moment, it feels cruel,
but it's the kindest thing we can do.
You don't text to ask if I made it home safe;
that's not your role to play as of 11:58.
And so the process of detangling ourselves from each
    other begins.
I cry as I cross off your favorite brand of coffee from my
    shopping list.
What starts as these frequent stabs of pain
evolves to a dull and gentle ache,
like when a mutual friend mentions your name
or I hear a lyric I know you'd hate.
And staying over here is how I show

I care for you.
And you giving me all this space is how
I know
you care for me, too.

Looking Up

I like to believe
that, on occasion,
we'll both have our faces
tilted up
seeing the same sky
at the same time.
Maybe that can be
enough.

The Waiting

You are not behind.
How unsurprising it should be
that our very different lives
will move at very different paces.
There's no line to cross by twenty-three
or thirty;
there's no box you have to check.
You're a completely unique person
with your own set of experiences.

All plants sprout and grow at different rates,
in different climates,
into different shapes.
What's buried deep inside the soil
may take a while to be seen.
And even then there are seasons it will not bloom.
Even then there are times it must be pruned.
Those times and seasons may vary between
someone else
and you.

And one more thing:
I'm so glad you have plans and dreams

to grow and love and create good things.
I also hope you don't forget
that life is not about to begin;
it's happening.
Right now,
it is happening.
And there is gold here
in the waiting.

Mistakes

There are times I get scared that I'll do something wrong,
so I don't do anything at all.
It's difficult to walk
when mistakes look like land mines,
and somewhere in my mind
that's what they'll become.
I'm still working on how to climb my way out of this one.
What's helped me greatly,
lately,
is remembering where
I've come from:

I've written hundreds of poems I hate,
and still not one has been a waste.
Maybe sometimes in order to create,
I have to get out what I don't want to say.
Maybe before words can be rearranged,
I have to sit down and put some on a page.

Maybe the worst mistake I ever could have made
was never even trying because
I was too afraid.

Hidden All Over

Whenever I feel lost,
looking desperately around
trying to figure out who I am,
I try to remember where I've been found:
in the six strings of my first guitar,
in an old friend's car,
in a field looking up at the stars,
in realizing I like the rain,
in an emergency room,
in a high school essay.
As I go through this list,
it occurs to me
that who I am is hidden all over
in people, in poetry,
in places, in books, in songs,
in falls, on roads, and in weeds.
I have not met every inch
of the person I've been
or the person I am
or the person I'll be.
I imagine me scattered about with the wind
where waiting to be discovered
are all my complexities.

So whenever I feel lost,
searching breathlessly up and down
trying to figure out who I am,
I try to remember that I will be found:
in a person that I haven't met,
in a place that I have never been,
in a poem that I haven't read,
in a song that hasn't been written
yet.
And when I come upon them,
I'll say, *Here I am.*
I found another piece.
Imagine just how many
are out there somewhere
waiting for me.

Miles

I fall in love with yellow things
like wildflowers and falling leaves
and lines that keep following
the pins stuck in my globe.
I'm not always sure what I should dream
because time is always changing things,
but know wherever my map leads
I do believe we'll grow.

The miles tell me we're breakable,
but the feeling is unmistakable,
so I learn to find some beauty in
headlights and radios.
I trail the moon between the trees;
I follow as it interweaves
the light with dark
until I finally turn onto your road.

I can feel so cut in half
existing in two photographs.
I never knew the word *goodbye*
could make me feel so cold.
But moments where our worlds collide

bring color to the black and white.
I never knew the miles my hands could span
to hold your own.

Sunday dies and Monday breathes
and faith lives in the in-between.
My passenger seat is empty,
and I sometimes feel alone,
but the trials of our circumstance
will never truly stand a chance
against the love we've fostered
and the fears that I've outgrown.

You are my home.

Autumn

The last night of summer
feels cooler this year.
We walk through the city
and hear people cheer
for the team on the screen
in the bar across the street.
I always feel pretty
in this shade of green.
Historically I hate
going on first dates,
and you say that I look surprised when I laugh.
You blush
when I say that *It's just,*
I wasn't expecting to have so much fun.
You walk me to my car,
and I plant my feet
so that I don't get swept up in
September breeze,
so that I don't reach cloud nine
or sink with the leaves.
But despite all my caution,
there's nothing
like loving somebody

in autumn.
You meet me at bookstores.
You make me black tea.
I wear your best sweaters.
Nobody wants flings
in September,
October,
November.
I meet your family one night in December.
You are good to me—
good enough to become what I see
in my dreams
the moment before I wake aching,
reliving the fading
from view.

There's nothing like loving somebody who
stops loving you.

October 5

I've not asked for much,
but I'm asking for this:
can I please hold on to October the fifth?
Can I keep that night just the way that it is?
You can do what you want with your version of it,
but can I leave it be
like I don't know the ending?
Can I hope at least then
you were not pretending?
In some other life,
I would stand at our wedding
and say that's the moment I knew.
It's not that I want you;
I'm smarter than that,
but I'm sick of everything
turning to ash.
Just this once,
can I keep the warmth
when the memory shows up at the door?
That's all.
Nothing more.

The Protagonist

If this is a movie,
I am not the true love;
I'm just the
conflict,
the roadblock,
the bad blood.
If this is a movie,
then no one's on my side.
I come up just short
of being the
bad guy.

If this is a story
you tell to your kids,
I imagine we aren't
all that serious.
If somebody asks
how the two of you met,
it's likely that I do not
even exist.

It takes me
one whole year and six months

to realize
that I am not the protagonist.

The fireworks fly,
you two finally unite,
and I doubt I'll ever trust
someone
again.

The People Who Hurt Us

My skin is dry and
the air is freezing and
my breath is sharp
when I see you leaning
against the car.
Remember when
we slid
into that tree?

I sink into your passenger seat,
and here it is.
No, not it—she.
I've asked; you've rolled your eyes and laughed.
At last, you want to be honest with me.

You whisper that you're sorry.
I whisper that I have to go.
You say, *Wait, give me a chance to explain*—
But actually, I really don't need to know.

Actually, I am grateful,
because now I have a reason to hate you.
It doesn't even wear

for six miles home,
fifteen steps to the front door,
eight more to the stairs,

and there
is where
the anger
is no longer
enough.
How cruel it is—
the capacity we have to miss
the people who hurt us.

When I Lay Down the Pen

I will bleed through the page
until I'm out of words.
I will explain my anger
and proclaim my hurt.
I will rework the lines
to best express my truth,
but when I lay down the pen,
I'll still miss you. When do
I stop missing you?

Hard Truths

I can put up a fight
for the rest of my life.
I can run. I can hide.
I'll still know.

I can choose to betray me
the rest of my days. See
the lie
and say, *That's right.*
I'll still know.

I can cry, beg, and plead—
scream, *No, I don't accept this*—
as if truth considers my personal preference.

I can go right on living
as if nothing's different,
but I can't just forget it.
I'll still know.

Halloween

I don't even have
to decorate
for Halloween this year.
There are ghosts that like
to hang
around the house.
If I'm not constantly on guard,
they'll surely tear me apart.
They are sneaky;
each one's quiet as
a mouse.
They hide in
socks that are not
    mine inside
the laundry.
They hide in
Polaroids I never threw
away.
They hide in
words that I wrote down
and never found
courage to say.

They bump my bruises,
open wounds, and
teach my heart new ways
to ache.

Between the Lines

I won't call you.
I won't send you Christmas cards.
I won't look you up on the internet
or write to ask you how you are,
and we won't catch up like old friends.
I won't be invited to your sister's wedding.
You won't be a place I can stay in the city
or an ICE contact
or a character reference,
but in my mind
for a split second
you'll still drive every little black car I see.
And when that song comes on the radio,
you'll be right there in my passenger seat.
You'll stay smiling in the pictures that I
print out just to hide,
and I'll make up stories to write my poems
but slip you there in the spaces between the lines.

The Beginning

You tell me,

You're just like the rain after a drought—

you take my face in your hands and my world turns inside
out—

*like a poem that the seas and trees and stars all got together
and wrote down.*

*I think I've been holding my breath and didn't realize until
now.*

Easy to Love

I'm bending and breaking.
I'm easy to love. I
can't look in the mirror.
I'm just what he wants.
I'm passing all his tests.
I love getting good grades.
I'm jumping through dog hoops.
I'm digging a deep grave.
I shrink beneath sweaters.
I shed all my skin.
I sink to the floorboards.
I'm rearranged by him.
My heart gets discarded.
She tugs on my sleeve.
Her eyes are accusing.
She asks, *What about me?*

This Is How Love Works

I told you exactly how to make me feel loved,
and I came to feel I was asking for too much,
but maybe it's just
after seven whole months,
you'd decided that you knew me better
than I knew
myself,
and I needed your guidance.
I needed your help,
and this is how love works:
you give and I take.
I say *please* and *thanks*
that I'm someone you're graciously willing to
tolerate.

The End

You tell me,
You are like a devastating flood—
like the faucet got left leaking and no one heard the water run.
You're like rain that I can't see through.
It's too much. I cannot breathe. You
walk away.
The parts of me that you once loved
you've come
to hate.

Seasons

He'll say that he loves her. He'll mean it.
He'll want her for more than a season.
She won't be a fling
or an *it's complicated.*
She'll say he's not like
other guys
that she's dated.

He'll grow into someone
who's ready to love.
He'll be
thoughtful and mature and
worthy of trust.
I will have been a test run,
a trial,
a lesson
he's learned.
Collateral damage.
A bridge that's been burned.

On the Urge to Isolate

The sky
will roar and scream and cry
and I
will not call her dramatic.
I will sit beneath the porch light
and watch clouds be
proudly
gray. Later I'll
look in the mirror
and, with lesson learned, refrain
from telling myself
that I cannot rain.
I do not have
to hide away.

I Try My Best

I try my best
to keep my head
above the water.
I buy the yellow flowers.
I play kind music in the shower.

I try my best
not to melt
too deep into the couch.
I take my thirty-minute walks.
I wave to all the neighbors' dogs.

I sign up for the gym,
and I go four times a week,
and I take care of my skin,
and I stop drinking caffeine,
and I wake up with the sun,
and I keep the kitchen clean.
I try not to come undone.
I try not to fall all the way down the sink.

I try my best
to believe that it's not permanent.

I try my best
to remember how time heals.
I try my best
to exist with this discomfort,
but the one thing I have not done
is allow myself
to feel.

As You Are

Allow yourself to be loved as you are
both in the light and in the dark—
all your failures and successes,
your whole broken, bandaged heart.
Allow yourself to be seen past
the caution tape and hard hats,
past the sea of bright green safety vests.
At your lowest.
At your best.

Too Sensitive

When I stopped trying to subdue
or otherwise apologize for who
I am, I began
to realize

some of those parts of me
I'd learned to label *weak*
were actually
my best things.

Expectations

I was not perfect.
You should not have expected me to be.
The fact you failed to love me well
has more to do with you than me.

Highs and Lows

When you gave me love,
it was
euphoric;
I could've had it
at the cost of
spending my life begging for it.

I Hope You're Happy

I hope that you are happy;
I hope I don't have to see it.
I hope you find your soul mate,
and I hope I never meet them.
I hope that you are better off,
and I hope that you never call,
and I hope all your dreams come true.
I really want the best for you.
I do not think the best includes

me.

Birthdays

You have a new girlfriend,
and I heard you think she's it.
You posted pictures for her birthday
the night she turned twenty-six
with a caption carefully composed
of words like
beautiful and *bright*.
When I turned twenty-two,
I sat by you
in the movie theater parking lot
and cried.
You told me I can't take a joke
and I was overreacting.
My birthday gift was thick skin,
but I don't remember asking.
I think I need to remind myself
it's a reflection of your growth
and not of my worth
that you can speak so highly of someone—
that you can put someone else first.

To Move On

You don't have to hurt someone
before you can move on.
I know it maybe feels that way,
but what would happen if you paused
and asked yourself,
will this bring closure?
Will this help to heal the cut?
Will the satisfaction last
(if it ever even shows up)?
Write the letter,
wait a month, then see
what you still think
is true.
When emotions somewhat settle,
decide then
what you should do.
You might come to find
that lashing out
is rubbing salt
in your own wound.
There are words we can't take back.
There are actions we can't undo.

Save Me

No one is coming to save me.
No one is coming to change me into some
lighter, kinder, braver, brighter
version of myself.
I must have imagined a million heroes
sitting alone at night in my room. I thought
if somebody came and believed in my dreams,
maybe then I could, too.
I never knew
how my heart would sigh in relief
or how I'd feel the earth shift beneath my two feet
the first time it finally occurred to me
that I am the one I've been waiting for.
My lungs released
the deep breath
they had been holding.
My shoulders fell.
My muscles relaxed.
I saw my reflection in the glass door,
and she said she loves me,
and I said it back.

Know and Love

May I never love who I could be (in theory)
more than who I actually am.
May I never sink teeth into a future so perfect
I exclude myself from the plan.
May I never attempt to abandon my strengths
in the name of taking up a little less space.
May I never put on a face that's so brave
I am actually proving how very afraid
I am
of disappointing the people around me,
of saying no,
of admitting I'm drowning,
of taking a break,
of walking away,
of appearing weak.
Instead, may I
breathe slowly
and take my time
and listen to my body, my heart, and my mind.
May I show up for myself—
broken, fractured, or bruised—
and may I love others like this—
with grace, patience, and truth.

Lose Something

Am I steeling for an end
that is
not coming?

Can I hold in my hands
something good
and not start sprinting
from it?

Am I really even
capable
of trusting?

Do I want to let you go,
or must I
lose something
to love it?

Panic Attacks

I feel it coming on again—
like no number of deep breaths in
could alter my trajectory,
like this path has been set for me.
I feel the control seep
from my fists down to my feet,
and I can't think,
and I can't speak.
I feel hot,
and I feel weak.
All the air exits my chest
and makes no promise of return.
There is an ocean in my ears.
I forget everything I've ever learned.
My eyes are seeing black,
and my heart is beating too fast,
and the worst part is
I don't know why.
I hoped
that last time
would be
the last time.

Beneath the Cloud

A window lights up
somewhere down the street.
You come outside—
clean hair and bare feet.
I am standing
soaked
beneath the cloud
that follows me.

I know I cannot pull you out from underneath,
but I could sit with you, at least,
and you don't have to speak.
You don't have to be anything.

You say these words, and nothing else,
and I am simply held.

Often, this is all it takes—
showing up as the world caves.

Swallow Me Up

Maybe somewhere
deep inside me,
I always knew it would come.
The perimeter of my heart
never could have
been enough.
Maybe I knew
one day I would
trip and fall and cease
to run—
that the storm was right
behind me,
ready to
swallow me up.

Underwater

I spend my whole December
underwater.
I do laps by the dim light
in the old YMCA.
I hope and pray
that I am not a disappointing daughter.
I go to my appointments,
and I promise I'll drive safe.
I'm healing;
it's not happening
as quickly as I'd like it to.
I still look in the mirror,
and I ask it,
Who the hell are you?
Remember when I
slept without the nightmares,
when I lived without the doubt?
What happened to her?
Where'd she go?
Where is she now?

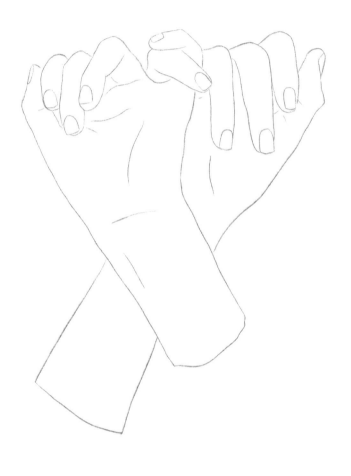

Twenty-three

I know I'm young; I feel like
I don't have the time to be.
Does everybody feel
this indistinct at twenty-three?
Where did all my edges go?
I used to think by now I'd know
where home is;
I thought that I'd have more friends.

I tell myself that I'll be fine,
but I don't believe me.
I feel discouraged when I have to
focus on my breathing.
I want to live out of a van.
I want to buy my own house.
I'm terrified to be alone.
I'm terrified to settle down.

Does it ever get better?
Is this feeling one that gets resolved?
Will I be able to unpack my bags
at my next stop?
Will twenty-four

bring any sort
of semblance of security,
or maybe, if not certainty,
then peace to live without it?

Run

Sometimes I get worried that my time is almost up—
like I've wasted all my wishes and I'm
running out of luck.
And people are going to see through it all now,
and I won't be able to ever explain how
I kept up the act for so long—
like, *Wow, what a show she put on.*
And I should have seen this coming, I guess,
because I've never been good
at letting good things rest;
I show up on the front porch in the middle of the night
and bang on the bottom of the screen door
looking for
a fight.
I know in my bones you are not here to stay,
so please, just leave.
Get it over with.
Go away.
Take it, and give it to somebody else.
I don't want it.
I don't want it.
I don't want it, I yell.
Of course I want it,

but I'm so afraid to lose it.
I'm worried that things happen to me
without me ever choosing them.
I'm worried life will pass by
without me ever having lived it,
because the whole entire time
I was bracing for the end of it.
It sounds ridiculous,
I'm aware,
but anxiety is a liar
whose very favorite pastime
is to spin me into spirals.
I'm still learning how to tell the difference
between my instinct—my knowing, my gut—
and that sense of unfounded urgency
usually pressing me
to run,
run,
run.

The Next Five Minutes

Rest in this:
what you're feeling is not permanent.
It may be powerful, painful, and scary,
but still completely
temporary.
And it might take a while to work through,
but there's no need to look that far ahead.
You can focus on
the next five minutes,
the next small step,
the next deep breath instead.
I am familiar with the lie—
that little voice in the back of my head
that says
it's never going to get better—
that awful feeling of hopelessness.
It has been there.
It has been strong;
it has been raging in wave after wave,
then it has settled.
The flood has subsided.
It has not stayed.
It did not happen overnight,

but I have come to find this
beautiful life.
Rest in this:
what you're feeling is not permanent.

You Still Did

Remember all the things
you swore you could not do
that you
still did.
Remember all the goals
you barely let yourself set
that you've
met.
Allow yourself
to wonder what's
the *best thing*
that could
happen.
Notice how
the world has yet
to end,
how your heart
has not ceased
to beat again.

The Small Steps

I promise you it matters—

your small step,
your deep breath,
your quiet *yes*
to choosing to find the light—
however dim—
and your awakening each day
to do it again.

You Are Safe

Relax your shoulders,
let your fingers fall from fists,
unclench your jaw,
and take a deep breath in.
Look around, and return to
the present.
Be here now.
Take some time to ground
yourself.
If you need it, ask for help.
You are safe.
You are loved.
Recognize how far you've come.

Homebody

I'm most at home
in my own body
when it's raining,
when I'm watering my plants,
when I'm writing,
when I'm painting,
when I dance,
when I'm holding up a book,
when I'm lying in the grass,
when I'm finding four-leaf clovers,
when I cry, and when I laugh.

I think it's lovely that
I never will have
fully learned myself;
I am complex. I am vast,
and this body where my soul dwells
will continue to discover
what it is that lets in peace
and love and light—
what it is that leads me home
after the long night.

Near You

It's been normal lately
to feel like myself
and not wish that I could be
somebody else.
I'm not acting or striving,
pretending or faking,
or stretching or shrinking,
or begging or chasing.
If I wrote a list
of things that are good,
I'd put falling asleep to rain
and feeling understood
and green tea and honey
and stories behind tattoos
and hearing your heart with
my arms wrapped around you.
It's there that the whole world falls away.
And I'm not extraordinary in any way;
I don't have exceptional gifts or fame,
but I love who I am today.

Patient Love

Your favorite book is filled now
with coffee-stained pages
from that time we ran inside
from the pouring rain and
I bumped into the table
as I reached to grab a blanket off the couch.
I covered up my mouth,
but you didn't mind.
And I felt peace there in your living room,
breathing in the scent of spilled coffee, rain, and you.
It didn't feel like temporary love
as you opened up the book
and told me, *Wait,*
I actually kind of like how this looks.
I rolled my eyes and laughed
and then looked down at your mismatched socks
and got this overwhelming feeling
that I really did belong.
But I once read we only really accept
the love that we think we deserve,
and the very next thought that came to me was,
This ending is going to hurt.
Because even as each stare between us

feels like kindness and patience,
sometimes my heart still tries to project
my past pain, all to keep me safe, but it
really just makes me anxious.
Because there's risk here either way.
I could pull the plug and run
and never know what could have happened
had I stayed.
But I'm choosing now to stay,
because I see the way you love me.
Though I know that things can change,
it's okay—
I'll be okay.
I'm relearning how to love,
and that is brave.

I Do Not Need You

I could love you
and lose you
and go right on living.
You could walk away now,
and my life would not end.
Light would still exist.
The planet would not cease to spin.
The sun would rise again and again.
I'd be sad and hurt and angry then
fine in the end.

I could love you
and lose you
and go right on living,
but I do not want to.
I have no interest in forgetting
the care that goes into your words
or the hope in your eyes,
that when you make me laugh there is pride in your smile,
that when you say you love me it is easy to believe you.
I do not need you,

and that is the best way I can think of to explain
how much I want you for every day
of the rest of my life
to have and to hold tight.
I want your heart. I want your mind.
I want the day that I met you
and the day we first kissed
and all the years it took for us to realize *this is it.*
This is what I choose. This is what I'm sure of.
This, I know, is love I do not ever want to let go of.

Finding My Balance

I can practice trusting myself
while maintaining awareness
that I'm not a mind reader.
Just because I think someone feels a certain way
does not automatically mean that they do.
I can practice trusting myself
while taking my anxiety
into consideration.
What seems like a gut feeling may be a fear
that dissipates once it is thought all the way through.

I don't want to overcorrect,
jumping from distrusting my mind
to thinking I always know best.
I don't always know best.
And it's not always easy—
stumbling along this pathway of healing.
Balance is complex.
Fortunately, there is no deadline in my life for finding it.
There is trial and error
and learning and growing.
Breaking and fixing.
Forgetting and knowing.

I'm here in the middle—
a great place to be—
where so much potential
just waits to be seen.
I can breathe deep and know
it's a safe place to rest.
I don't need to have it figured out just yet.

A Poem for the People I Love

May your heart and your brain take time
to listen to each other.
May your beautiful mind
remain a kind place to be.
May your smile arrive
at its own pace
on its own terms.
May your eyes rain
as often as they
need.
May your body feel nourished.
May your soul feel well rested.
Wherever your feet are planted,
there in that space may you be present.
May all your decisions be guided
by love and light
instead of fear.
And may you know
that wherever the wind blows you,
I am right here.

Light Source

Pay attention to
what you're doing,
where you are,
and who you're with
in moments
when the light starts streaming in—
when the weight, inch by inch, lifts.

Vows

I will communicate my desires
rather than hold you to
unspoken expectations.
I will seek to love you
in both of our languages.
How lucky am I
that one day
like a film, my life
will flash before
my eyes,
and you'll fill countless frames—
my great love,
my deep breath,
my clean slate.

Home

I know you will grow.
I know you will flow into
someone that I don't know now,
but I will know then.
I know there will be parts of you that erode
with the rain and the waves and the wind.

I know you'll evolve;
that's what people do.
My heart will make space to
accommodate you.
You don't have to stay in one shape
for my love to remain.
Please feel free to always be completely you.

My hope for us
is that we build a home
where we each feel safe
to fail or change or bloom.

I am not certain of very much.

I am certain about you.

The Life I Dream Of

I dream of a life that's full of
wind chimes
and rain storms
and mornings on the porch
and playlists
and gardens
and big stacks of books,
of poems
and coffee
and dancing while we cook,
of family dinners,
hearing thunder late at night,
open blinds,
evening walks,
losing track of time while we talk,
taking breaks,
Saturdays,
the time of day when light falls just right
    in the
living room.
I never knew
I'd be so grateful

for such simple things.
It does not take a lot, it seems—
it's not like what I thought,
   I think.

On Time

In certain seasons,
I've worried
I was moving too quickly or slowly,

but these days
I worry less
knowing

I've always arrived
exactly on time
for my life.

Nothing that's
meant to be mine
will pass me by.

How Do You Know?

It isn't a lot of things
that I thought it would be.
I assumed I would sense it was
    happening
immediately,
but no.
The fall was sort of slow,

like I started on a walk with him
and looked at a map somewhere
    during it
and realized, *Wow, we've really
    dropped in elevation,*
and I just sort of clumsily threw
    that into our conversation.

He smiled and said,
I love you, too.
*I could honestly, confidently, get
    your name tattooed.*
He is a safe space
and a deep breath

and while I pace the kitchen
he stands at the stove and he says
all the right things
to help me climb down from my head.

And a part of my heart
moves outside of my chest.

You Are Growing

I think a lot about what I might say to my younger self,
but not what my older self might say to me.
And in the latter prompt,
there's obviously not
quite as much certainty, but
I think maybe she'd say,
Your opinion on your own art will change
a million times,
but I am grateful now for every word you write,
because you're learning with every line.

And I'm hopeful she'd add,
I know that,
sometimes,
you get really sad.
But keep your heart open,
and trust that ahead of you
there is so much light.

And maybe she'd tell me,
some of those stages you are tempted to rush through
are stages I miss.
Some of them benefit from a bit of perspective,

but some of them ask
you just to slow down
and notice.

There are so many people who will love you
and whom you will love so deeply in return.
There are sunsets
and mountains
and waterfalls to see;
there are poems to write
and lyrics to learn.

It isn't all golden
and good
and beautiful,
but you'd be surprised
by how much of it is.

Be kind.
Have patience.
Rest and live
in this uncertainty
and openness.
Hey, they matter—
those seeds that you're sowing.

You are growing.
You are growing.
You are growing.

Better Days

Better days will come.
Presently, I'm not sure
how or when,
but something deep within me trusts
I'll feel the sun rest on my skin
again.

I acknowledge this
as progress—
knowing light will return still.
With every wave that's passed,
I've learned it always has
and always will.

Pockets of Light

I used to think I was
completely past it.
And maybe one day that will be true,
but until then

I'll find the
pockets of light
even here, even now
with the impending rain;
with the clouds
overhead;
with the bad days and bad dreams and dread;
with the anxious thoughts
bouncing off
walls in my head.

I'll find the
cracks in the concrete
where flowers grow through,
never forcing myself to
believe what's not true,
but trusting the sun will certainly
come up soon,

be it next week
or next month
or next June.

And I'll learn some
way to create light
in case I
can't find it.
And I'll read this poem
when I need to be reminded
of the promise I've made to myself.
No, I am *not* alone.
Yes, I *can* ask for help.

Idyllic

I know I will look back and
be so incredibly
grateful for this exact
version of me,
who is scared out of her mind,
who just wants to *sleep*,
who is grasping at light like
she needs it to breathe,
who is messy and hopeful
and often quite blue.
This part's not idyllic.
This part matters, too.

Reflections

One day, I will die.
And while I
won't be there to see my funeral,
there are a few things that I have become
pretty certain of:

No one will stand at the front
and say,
Let's remember the color and cut
of her hair and the way
it fell and framed her face.
No one will reflect on my height or
    my weight.
No one will laugh or weep
while delivering their speech
on the size of my waist
or the shade of my teeth.

I know this,
because when I think of the people I love,
those are the last things that come
to my mind.

Instead, I think of
patience and
kindness and
humor and
wisdom and
cosmic capacities for grace.
I think of days where I forget what anyone was wearing,
but I still feel the smile that was on my face.

I am so guilty of getting it backward
and feeling as if the way I look is the most
meaningful and interesting part of me,
but still, I will keep coming back to the truth:

Those things that make days
and give life
and spread that good, bright, beautiful light—

those are things my mirror
will never be able
to reflect.

Be Kind to Yourself

I hope today you remember that
the sky is not humiliated by its vastness,
and the mountains remain unashamed of their height.
Mother Earth and her oceans are not afraid of their size,
and the sun is not concerned if someone has to squint
    their eyes—
it will shine.
And it will not apologize for
its light.
And like the trees teach us that it's okay
to lose our leaves as seasons change
and then come back to life,
I hope that nature teaches us to look at ourselves and
be kind.
I hope that we don't dim or shrink or fold into spaces far
    too tight.
Yes, today I hope you look at yourself and
you are kind.

Acknowledgments

About two years ago, I began sharing my poetry. In the time since then, I have watched so many of my dreams I barely had the courage to believe in come true. I feel so lucky to have so many people to thank for that.

Thank you to Haley Heidemann for your work and guidance throughout this entire process. You believed in me as a writer, and I will be appreciative of that forever.

To my editor, Sarah Cantin, and the incredible team at St. Martin's Press: Thank you for all the work you have done to bring this book to life. I have felt safe and supported every step of the way, and that is because of you!

Thank you to Chloe Purpero Johnson for providing illustrations that exceeded my highest hopes. Your art is so special, and I am honored to have it featured alongside my words.

Thank you to all the friends both online and off who have supported me as I've written and shared my poems. I wish I could explain how much your kindness means to me.

To my parents and my family, thank you for encouraging my creativity; I've found your faces in every audience I've ever been in front of. Beyond that, your love has remained steady and constant my whole entire life. I won't ever be able to thank you enough for that, so I'll just say I love you, too.

Thank you to my husband, Spencer, for everything; if I try to write it all down, I think I'll run out of pages. I love you so much. I'm happy you convinced me to not delete that post.

About the Author

SOPHIE DIENER is a writer based in the Midwest. She writes and shares poetry about mental health, body image, love, and heartbreak. *Someone Somewhere Maybe* is her first book.